HERE COMES WHISKERS

JO ROBINSON

Printed in the United States of America

ISBN: 978-1-963068-03-0 (sc)
ISBN: 978-1-963068-13-9(e)

History
2023.12.20

Table of Contents

Chapter 1

Bill and Sandy

It was a beautiful spring morning. Gentle breezes, birds singing, and best of all, it was Saturday. Saturday, the day Bill loved the most. He remembered when he was a child, he looked forward to Saturdays. Mom and Dad would be sitting at the kitchen table, drinking their morning coffee, while he lay on the living room floor watching cartoons. He loved those memories. And he still loved Saturdays, even though now he's sitting at the table, reading the Saturday morning paper instead of watching cartoons. Sandy, his wife, had just finished brewing a pot of coffee. The aroma filled the kitchen as they sat down together. Sandy had picked up her favorite magazine that had just arrived the day before, and Bill reached for newspaper. After a few minutes, Bill said, "they've got baby chicks for sale at the hardware store." Sandy looked up from her magazine and said "Hmm." and went back to her magazine. But Bill kept reading the ad. Sandy peeked over the top of the magazine, watching him. Hoping he would talk about something else he had just read, but instead, Bill put down the newspaper, took a sip of his coffee and said, "Sandy? Why don't we go to town and get us some baby chicks?" Sandy looked quite surprised. He had her full attention now. "What on Earth are we going to do with baby chicks?" She asked. "Where are we going to put them? Do you know anything about raising baby chicks?" Bill answered her saying, "how hard could it be?" with a big grin on his face. "we'll pick up some supplies while we're there. I know they will show us everything we need." Sandy sat there like a frozen statue, never blinking, waiting for him to say, "just kidding". But those two words never came. Bill started wiggling his feet into his shoes and picked up his keys from the counter. Then he stood by the door as if waiting for Sandy to do the same. For a brief moment Sandy just sat there, still holding her magazine in her hands. Then she slowly stood up and slipped her feet into her shoes and walked towards Bill. Next thing she knew, they were in the car and heading to the hardware store.

Chapter 2

Bill was like a kid in a candy store. His head was whipping from left to right as he walked through the isles. When he finally arrived at the back of the building, there he saw them. Large silver bins with heat lamps hanging over each one and the sounds of chirping coming from everywhere. He stood there for a moment, taking it all in, then slowly approached the first container. His eyes got big and so did his smile as he looked at the tiny round balls of fluffs with feet. "May I help you?" Bill jumped backwards when he heard this and nearly knocked Sandy over. He hadn't noticed the man in the red vest standing beside him. Bill quickly composed himself. "I'm Jason" the man continued. "See anything you like?" "Oh, yes! I'm looking to buy a baby chick." "Well, there's is a minimum purchase of six chicks." The man replied. Sandy felt a slight whimper escape her throat. Bill's grin got wider. "Well Jason, I guess we will take six." Twenty minutes later, and a cart full of feeders, waterers, heating bulbs and chick feed, Bill and Sandy made their way to the front of the store and to the checkout counter. Bill couldn't remember what kind of chicks he had bought, even though it's only been minutes since he had picked his out. Jason had gotten him so confused when he asked Bill if he wanted cockerels in the mix. Bill, not knowing what a cockerel was had said "all six would be great". Jason chuckled and explained that cockerels were roosters, and they would probably want some hens to go with them. Bill thought, "okay, one confused moment. That's to be expected I guess" But Jason's next question was more of a challenge. "What kind of chicks would you like?" Bill didn't want to appear totally stupid about the subject, so instead he said, "What kind do you have?" "Well, we got Black Copper Marans, Blue Easter Eggers, Orpingtons, Barred Rock, Australorp" Bill didn't know what to say. "Over here we have Sumatras Blue laced Red Wyadotte's. Black Silkes, and some Ameraucana's". Okay, now Bill was feeling the pressure. Especially feeling Sandy's eyes on him. He even thought he heard snickering coming from her. "Sandy, dear. I'll let you pick out what chicks you want." Sandy immediately stepped forward, and with all the confidence he knew she had, picked out five hens, or pullets, and one cockerel. "She makes it look so easy." He thought.

Once in the car, Sandy felt a twinge of excitement as she held the little box in her lap, listening to the sounds of chirping coming from inside. They were awfully cute. She loves little baby animals. Maybe this wasn't going to be so bad. Maybe this was going to be fun after all. While they were driving home, she gazed out the car window and imagined fresh eggs in the morning and being able to look out her back window and see chickens in the yard. The perfect country scene. She had no idea what she was in for.

Chapter 3

Upon arriving in their driveway, their neighbor, Hank, approached them with a bucket full of fresh tomatoes he had just picked from his garden. "What's that you got there?"

"We decided to get some chickens" Bill said with that same old grin. Hank just nodded. Hank had been a farmer since he was sitting on his grandpa's lap. He was considered to be the best farmer in the county. "Well, let me see what you got" Sandy was eager to open up the little box and show him the little fluffs. She said, "aren't they the cutest things?" Hank just grinned at her. "Do you have a chicken coop ready to go for them?" Bill's big smile froze on his face in an awkward position. "Um, well, no. Hadn't gotten that far yet."

"No problem" said Hank, They're not quite ready for that anyway. I can help you build one if you'd like." The three of them went into the house to look at different types of chicken coops. Hank was getting a little concerned about the baby chicks and said "don't you think you need to get them out of that little box and under a heat lamp?" Confusion set in again with Bill, but Sandy got right up, went to the supplies they had bought at the hardware store and in no time the babies were all set with food and water. And the heat lamp over them felt good. The babies went right to fresh water and food. Bill's nerves relaxed a little bit. He thought, well that wasn't so hard.

After they decided on a coop that looked suitable, Hank started writing down all the materials and hardware they were going to need to build it. Sweat beads started forming on Bill's forehead. This little project was becoming a bit pricy. But he wasn't going to let this discourage him. It was just part of the planning he hadn't considered. Sandy began to start fixing supper while Hank and Bill went back to the hardware store. Forty-five minutes later they arrived back home and started unloading lumber and hardware. Hank said, "I'll be back first thing in the morning, and we'll get this thing built for you really quick". When Hank left, Bill and Sandy started to relax and enjoy watching the babies. "What are we going to name them"? Sandy asked" "Good question" Bill replied. Bill knew that they had 5 little girls and one little boy. One of the little girls was smaller than the others. Sandy reached down and picked her up and cuddled her. The baby chick seemed to enjoy it and even seemed to take to Sandy. "Look at the little puffs on her cheeks. I'm naming this one Whiskers". Sandy felt her heart melting as she held little Whiskers. The small rooster became Rocky, and the others were Buffy, Little Red, Buttons, and Dottie.

By the end of the week so much progress had been completed. A nice chicken coop was now in the backyard with a fence around it. Sandy wanted to make sure they had plenty of room to walk around in. The baby chicks still weren't able to be left out there alone for very long because Sandy knew they would get cold, and they weren't able to get up the ramp and into the coop on their own just yet. So, Sandy decided that they would be outside for 30 minutes at a time and then right back inside with the heat lamp on them. But it wasn't long before the chicks wanted to stay outside, and they even started going inside the coop on their own where the food and water was kept. Sandy continued to check on them every night before they went to bed. And every time she would see them sitting on their little roosts that Bill and Hank had built for them, sleeping peacefully.

It wasn't long before they were halfway grown. When Sandy would go to the pen to give them treats, Whiskers would come up to the fence to greet her. Sandy would reach down and pick her up. It was a special time for them. It was cuddle time.

But one dark night, all that changed. Tragedy happened. Sandy went out to feed her young chickens and when she got halfway there, she saw the gate was open! Sandy just froze. There were no chickens in sight. Her head whipped from left to right and back left again. Then she screamed for Bill to come out. The door busted open wide as he bolted out the house knowing something was terribly wrong. "They're gone! They're gone!" Bill ran a few steps to the left then a few steps to the right and then he ran towards the back of the property where the woods begin. The whole time he was calling "Chicken! Chicken!" But there were no chickens. Bill and Sandy searched up and down the road and into the woods, looking for any signs of them. But there was nothing to be found. "Where did they go? What's happened to them? They couldn't have just vanished!" Sandy was in tears. Bill looked at the gate. No, they hadn't vanished. They were stolen. Finally, the sun set, and they were forced to be inside, still not knowing where their chickens were. Bill and Sandy sat quietly before they went to bed.

There were no words to be said. All they could do was wait, hope, and pray that their chickens would either make their way back home, or be found. Even before the sun came up the next morning, Bill went out to see if they had come home, but all he saw was Sandy standing at the edge of the yard looking towards the wooded area, tears running down her face. He walked up to her and put his arm around her shoulder to comfort her. "I just don't know what's happened" she said "Where are they? Where did they go? Are they OK?" She looked up into Bill's eyes and said, "are they OK? Did they get cold last night?" Bill wrapped his other arm around her and held her tight as she cried on his chest. Tears were falling from Bill's eyes too.

By the end of the second week, they stopped going out looking for the chickens. They knew they weren't there. If only they knew what happened, it would be some form of closure. But not knowing where they are or if they're OK was what was tearing Bill and Sandy up inside. The chickens had been part of their family. They had become so attached to them. Sandy kept herself busy as best she could, but her mind kept going back to Whiskers and the others. About how Whiskers would come up to the fence, wanting to be picked up. Always wanting to be cuddled. Where was Whiskers now?

Chapter 4

Whiskers

The end of the day was drawing near. Whiskers and her friends were gathering around the coop door, preening themselves, getting ready to go to sleep. Last few bites of food, a few more sips of water, then into the coop to find their favorite branch to roost on. Whiskers liked the top level the best. That's where she could look out the window and enjoy the night air. In no time at all, she was asleep, along with the other young hens and Rocky.

She suddenly woke up with a start when she heard her friends squawking loudly. Then the squawking turned into more of a scream. That's when she felt two large hands grab her from overhead, snatching her off her perch. Whiskers was used to being picked up. Sandy picked her up every day. But this wasn't Sandy. These were rough hands. Hands that squeezed too hard. She felt herself squawking too. In an instant she was shoved into a wire cage along with two others. She could hear the remainder that were still in the coop cry out in surprise and fear as they too were being grabbed. All six had been crammed in the cage. They couldn't have fit another chicken in there if they tried.

The man who had stolen Sandy and Bill's chickens threw the cage in the back of his pickup and was speeding down the highway. He knew he could make some money from these chickens. When he pulled into his driveway, he grabbed the cage and started walking towards his backyard. He opened the cage and unceremoniously dumped all the chickens in the pen then went into his house. Whiskers and the other chickens were still dazed and confused. They stayed huddled together. It was the only thing that was familiar to them. And that's how they were the next morning when that man came back out. He placed a bowl of water on the ground and threw some breadcrumbs at them. Then he went back into the house.

There was no shelter or coop for them to go into, just a fence around them. The bread was gone in no time, so they tried to find bugs to fill their tummies. Day turned into night, and they sat close together again for warmth and comfort. But it was at that moment a clap of thunder could be heard and the rain started coming down. And it kept raining. It continued to rain the rest of the night. There was no way to get out of it, no coop to go into, so they stood in the corner and endured it. Whiskers was so cold and so wet. She started to shiver along with the others. Whiskers thought of home. Home! Where there was plenty of food and plenty of shelter. And where Sandy and Bill were. Home! Where Sandy would pick her up and cuddle her. Where she felt safe and loved. Home! She just wanted to go home.

Chapter 5

Bill and Sandy

Right about the time Bill and Sandy sat down to have their evening meal, there was a knock on the door. Bill rose from his chair and opened it. "Hank! What a pleasant surprise! Come on in. Have you had supper yet?" "Thanks, but that's not why I'm here. You see, from what I recall, I think I saw your chickens yesterday. They were being sold at the auction barn the next county over" Sandy jumped out of her chair and joined the two men. "You saw them???" Sandy said. Excitement was in her voice. "Where are they?" "Who brought them in?" "Did you get them?" "Who has them now?" "Where are they?"

"Whoa" Hank held up one hand to make the point. "One question at a time" Bill felt Sandy's hand slip in his. "I don't know who brought them in, or who bought them. I got there later, after the small animals were already sold. I was trying to find another heifer. And as I was loading her in the trailer, I looked over and saw what I think was your chickens. They were outside waiting for the new owner to pay and load them up. When I finished loading the heifer, I went back to see if they were in fact your chickens. But the buyer had already left with them." Sandy put her hand to her heart and gasped. That was the first piece of good news they'd had regarding her stolen chickens. Even though they were still lost, they now had a place to start in finding them.

The next weekend found Bill and Hank at the auction barn. They didn't know exactly how they were going to find answers, but they figured they would just follow their instincts. "I'm sure the people working here can't give out personal information, but it's a place to start. We can get a bidding number at the same time," said Hank. "Lead the way," Bill said, and he followed Hank to the window. Sure enough, they didn't get any answers from the lady behind the window. "Do you know how many people bring chickens here to sell every week? Probably close to 50! I'm not able to give you that information, nor would I have the time to sort out chicken sellers from those who were selling something else. NEXT!" The men picked up their bidding card and stepped out of line. "Well, that went well," Bill chuckled. Hank grinned in agreement. "Let's find a seat and maybe we can talk to some guys." Three men who worked there were bringing out cages of small animals and setting them in groups to be auctioned. There were not only chickens, but rabbits, quail, turkeys, guineas, and even two peacocks, all of which were squawking, screeching, or crowing. They found two available seats close to a group of men. Hank, being a very sociable man, enjoyed talking to people and joined right in as if he'd known them for years. Bill was taking it all in, all the animals and all the people. One thing for sure, it was really loud! But not loud enough for him to not be able to pick up on what Hank was saying. "There were six young chickens sold here last week" he said to the men, "does any of you know who might have bought them? They were all in the same cage" then he described them as much as he could. "I might know who bought them," an older man said. "Let me think of that guy's name." At that moment Hank and Bill both caught sight of a man getting up quickly and leaving the area. Hank said, "I'll be right back" and took off after him. Bill wasn't sure what to do. Stay here and see if he could get more information from these men or follow Hank. He decided Hank could take care of things on his end, and he would see what he could find out on his.

Hank hurried out the barn trying to catch up with the suspicious man, but as he stepped out into the sunlight, the stranger was nowhere to be found. He scanned the parking lot when he noticed an old, beat-up gray pickup truck slinging gravel and dirt as it left the lot. It was too far away from Hank to see who was driving, but the driver seemed to be in a hurry to leave. Hank couldn't see the license plate, but he made a note of every detail he could see on the truck. Toolbox in the truck bed, shotgun in the back window, trailer hitch, missing a back bumper and a dent in the driver's side door. "Second place to start" he said to himself and went back in the auction barn. Bill was still sitting there totally involved in the conversation. He lowered himself beside Bill and asked if he'd learned anything so far. "I have" he said, "no one here knows who brought them in, but they have an idea who bought them. Also, they suggested we go to the guys in the back who check animals in and talk to them." "let's go" Hank said as he rose off the bench. As they walked to the back, Bill told Hank that the person who bought them just lives down the road. He had a description of the farm too. "We'll go there after we talk to these guys." Bill nodded. Bill was surprised at how many animals there were. Several cages of chickens and other small animals. Stalls were erected along the side and back walls and were occupied by horses, cattle, and donkeys. Hank talked to the men who was busy moving all the animals. Only one man stepped forward with more precise information. I've seen him come in here before. Several times. His last name is Jackson. I'm not sure what his first name is. Hank and Bill thanked the men and left. "Let's see if we can find that house."

As they pulled into the driveway where they figured the chicken buyer lived, a lady came out to greet them. The men introduced themselves and explained the reason they came by. "Yes" the lady said, "My husband did buy some chickens last week." Bill's knees almost buckled with hope. "May I see them?" Bill said with a quivering voice. "Well, you see, they're not here" Bill went from extreme joy to extreme discouragement. "I don't think my heart can take much more of this" he thought. "Let me give my husband a call. He can tell you where they are." She turned and went back to the house. Minutes later, she returned with a pleasant smile on her face and a piece of paper in her hand. "This is where they are now" she said. "A friend of my husband was wanting some chickens and asked him if he would get her some." But before she handed Hank the piece of paper, she pulled her hand back and said, "why are you looking for these chickens?" Now her sweet face turned into one of suspicion. "They were stolen from my place a couple of weeks ago." Bill's face was void of all expression. "Lands sakes alive!" she said, putting her hand on her heart. "I promise you; he did not know those chickens were stolen! He would never have bought them if he did!" Hank raised his hands. "Oh no ma'am. I know full well no one knew. We're just trying to track them down and get them back to Bill here and his wife." After she handed Hank the piece of paper with the address, she offered them to come in and have a glass of sweet tea, but they explained they had to be moving on. The men thanked her and got back in the truck.

"You want to go by this house now, or do you want to wait and get some rest first?" "No, I'm fine. If it's okay with you, I'd like to visit this address and see if they are there. There's nothing more I'd like to do today than go home and present the babies to Sandy. Hank nodded and backed out of the driveway and started in the direction of the next house.

Chapter 6

Whiskers

The next morning the man came out to check on them and throw them more bread. It seemed like he didn't care what happened to them. And dirt was getting on her food!

Three days later he returned to the pen, but this time it was not to feed them, but to catch them. The pen was so small, it didn't take him very long to get them all back in the wire cage. He thew the cage in the back of his truck again and drove off. The man was heading to the auction barn!

Once he arrived, he unloaded the cage and left. Whiskers could see other chickens in wire cages. They looked as miserable as she was.

Hours passed. The auction started. Announcements of the rules and payment options were quickly made clear to the buyers. Then one at a time the cages were set on the front table, or a man would walk around the arena with them so people could have a better look. Shortly after that, they were taken away. When Whiskers saw them come to her cage, she stood up to get a better look at things. She was desperate to see Sandy or Bill in the crowd. But she didn't see them. All she knew was she didn't want to go back to that mean man's place. She didn't see him in the crowd either. That was good. Suddenly a man yelled, "SOLD!" and the mallet hit the table, making her jump and squawk. Off they went again to another part of the barn. This time they were near the door and the sun was shining on them. Whiskers became so hot, along with the other chickens with her. She hadn't had anything to drink for so long. Soon, to her relief, a family picked them up and started for their car. Once there they begin transferring the chickens from the wire cage to a cage they had brought. Whiskers realized she might have a chance to escape, so she prepared herself to make a run for it. She looked over at Buffy and Little Red. They knew what she was thinking, and they had the same idea. When Dottie was being removed, Whiskers made her move. She exploded out of the cage, flapping her wings as hard as she could, and squawking loudly. In all the chaos, everyone was trying to catch her, grabbing at anything they could. Her legs, her wings, even her tail. But Whiskers got away, leaving a few tail feathers in the man's hands. She gave one quick look back and to her surprise, there was Buffy and Little Red. They had also gotten away while the people were trying to catch Whiskers and were right behind her. They ran/flew as long as they could. When they were too tired to keep going, the three stopped and looked around. They were surprised at how far they had gotten. They could no longer see the barn or the people. They stood there for a while, catching their breath, trying to figure out what they were going to do next.

Chapter 7

Bill and Hank

The house was set off the road several yards, but it was clear this was the one. The men could see a large chicken coop sticking out from behind the car port. Bill recognized two of his hens immediately. "THAT'S THEM! THAT'S THEM!" Bill yelled as he pointed towards the windshield. Hank gave the truck a little more gas and they were at the top of the driveway in no time. Bill jumped out and almost lost his footing before running towards the coop. There was no stopping him. A big man stepped out of the house and looked glaringly at Bill. "Hey! Where you think you're going??" He boomed. Immediately Hank stepped up to him and started filling him in on why they were there. Hank was a tall man, about 6', but he had to raise his head to look this man in the eye. He quickly started explaining the situation, but the man wasn't looking at him. He had his eyes fixed on Bill, and he didn't look so happy. In about three strides he was standing next to Bill. "I said what you doing here?" That was when Bill turned and jumped back. "Um, um," stammered Bill. His voice was quivering as well as his legs. Again, Hank stepped up and tried to explain. Bill made one slight shift to put Hank between himself and this big man who looked like he could cut down a huge tree without breaking a sweat. In Hank's slow, easygoing way of speaking, he continued explaining the circumstances. "So, you see, we're here to see if Bill's chickens would happen to be here". Hank turned his head to acknowledge Bill, but almost didn't see him. He had to turn farther, and there he was. A grin slipped across Hank's face. "Teddy? Who's that you're talking to?" "Teddy?" thought Bill. "This big guy's name is 'Teddy?'". The man named 'Teddy' snapped his head back towards Bill and had a 'Don't you dare!' look on his face. A petite lady came out the back door and approached the men, followed by two little girls with sunshine hair. The little girls ran to their daddy who immediately swooped them both up with one quick motion, and with one big arm. "He doesn't look so mean and scary now" Bill thought. "He looks more like 6'3" 275 pound marshmallow"

After the nerve-racking beginning, things finally smoothed out and everyone was more relaxed. Bill was even able to form full sentences. "So, I have stolen chickens" Teddy said. "I guess you're wanting them back". With all honesty Bill said, "I will pay you double, no...triple what you paid for them." "I guess it's the right thing to do" the wife said. Teddy gently lowered his daughter's and walked over to the chicken coop where several chickens were pecking the grass. "which ones are yours?" Bill looked at all the chickens, but only saw three that he recognized. "Just these three. Are there anymore? Maybe in the coop?" "Nope, that's all of them". Ms. wife tapped Teddy on the arm, "you remember? Three got loose when we were loading them up" "Oh, that's right. I don't know where they're at. I guess you could say they flew the coop" and Teddy busted out laughing, being quite amused at his own witty sense of humor. Bill didn't see any humor in it at all. How could he feel so happy and so upset all at the same time? Ms. wife went back into the house and returned with a cardboard box. "Here. Put them in this". She handed it to her husband. Bill could tell his babies had changed. They seemed skittish and nervous. No wonder. He couldn't imagine what all they had been through the last couple of weeks. Sandy will change all that. Once they were home, where they belonged.

Chapter 8

Whiskers

Whiskers, Buffy, and Little Red had made the great escape. But now what? After a long rest, they started walking, even though they weren't sure where they were going. Anywhere but that old barn! Whiskers had a sudden sense of urgency of being out in the open, where someone could see them and catch them. She scurried to the end of the open field and into a field of soybeans. There was plenty of food to eat, but she sure would like to have some cool fresh water. As night drew near, they found a quiet place to stop and sleep. And it didn't take long for them to do so. The next morning Whiskers felt something nudge her. She figured it was Buffy. Buffy was always pushing up against her. Wait! There it was again! But Buffy was on her other side. Whiskers jumped with a start, and so did the baby deer. Now all four were staring at each other, not knowing what to do. The fawn lowered her head and bumped Whiskers again. None of the chickens felt fear, only curiosity. The mother of the fawn stepped up beside her baby. "Whoa" thought Whiskers. "That's a big one!"

It seemed as if the mother was smiling at Whiskers. She nudged her baby away and they went off into the wooded area just past the bean field. Not knowing what else to do, the three chickens followed them. Mom and baby grazed as they walked through the trees. Then they suddenly disappeared down a small slope. Whiskers, being the curious one, sped up to see where they went. As she approached the top of the slope, she could see what mom and baby were doing. Oh joy! They were drinking from a creek! They ran down the slope to join the deer. They couldn't get there fast enough. Cool, fresh water! It never tasted so good. Mom and baby went on their way while the chickens kept drinking. They knew they had to keep moving. Somehow, they had to find their way back home.

Chapter 9

Bill and Sandy

Sandy heard Hank's truck coming up the driveway. They had been to the auction since early this morning to see if they could find out who bought her babies, but it was almost dark now. She knew they had been doing more other than being at the auction barn. She went to the door to meet them. But as she watched Bill get out of the truck holding a cardboard box and grinning from ear to ear, her heart started racing. "You found them!" she said. "Well, we found three of them." She ran to meet Bill halfway, eager to see which ones he had. They went to the chicken pen to let them out. As Bill opened the box, Sandy reached in and lifted up Dottie. She held her for a long time before setting her down. Then she reached in the box again and lifted Rocky. He seemed to be extremely nervous. She set him down without the cuddles. Last chicken. Was it Whiskers? Her heart sank when she saw it was Buttons, even though she was glad Buttons was back home, but that meant Whiskers was still lost. Poor Buttons. She pushed her head up against Sandy's neck. Sandy could feel her little body shaking. She held her for several minutes before setting her down. They all had gone over to the feeder and waterer. They were acting like they hadn't eaten or drank since they disappeared. Even though three were still missing, Sandy had hopes they would find their way back home.

Chapter 10

Whiskers

Well rested and refueled, the three chickens continued on their journey. It became too difficult to stay in the woods, so they found a road and walked along side it. Several times cars would go past them so fast that they were blown off the road and into the ditch. A couple of times, the car would stop. Someone would get out and try to catch them, but they were too smart for that. They had learned how to do a run/fly, covering a large amount of ground in no time flat. They followed the road until they came across a small town. They kept an eye out for people wanting to snatch them up. Then Whiskers noticed a man loading fresh produce in the back of his truck. She sure would like to nibble on those tomatoes, she thought. They quickly made their way to the truck where the tailgate was down, and promptly hopped in. The man didn't notice he had free loaders in the back before he drove off. Whiskers was enjoying her meal when it was quickly interrupted by the truck moving. Flashbacks flooded her memory of the night that mean man took them from their coop. All the chickens could do now was squat down and try not to be bounced or blown off. The trip didn't take too long before it arrived at its destination. They were at a farmer's market. When the man got out of his truck and was ready to unload his produce, he noticed three chickens there too. With a swift swing of his arm, he yelled, "get outa here!" and they did just that.

Chapter 11

Bill and Hank

One of the things Bill enjoyed was going to Paducah to the farmer's market. They didn't have a garden, but they loved home grown vegetables and fruits. This was the way to help farmers and get fresh food for themselves. Hank drove this time. As they strolled along the walkway they would stop at people's booths and pick out what they wanted. This time though, something caught Bill's eye. "Was that a chicken I just saw?" But it was gone just that fast. "Maybe it was a dog", he thought. And he went back to his shopping.

At the same time Bill caught a glimpse in the corner of his eye, Whiskers heard a familiar voice. She stopped and looked around for the source, when suddenly someone tried to grab her. The three chickens took off running.

They would never be taken by someone again. They were going home. But she was wrong. She felt hands on her. And more people were chasing Little Red and Buffy. In no time, the three were in a car, and were leaving, going to who knows where.

Chapter 12

Whiskers

They rode for several miles, sitting on children's laps and being patted. Whiskers realized that even though they are strangers, they seemed nice. They were gentle with the chickens. It was the next best thing to being with Sandy. When the car stopped, the children gently carried them to a pen where there was food and water. And a coop! A nice clean, dry coop. When night came upon them, Whiskers just couldn't let herself go in the coop. She laid down by the gate instead. She missed her owners so much. The next morning the same children came running out of the house and up to the pen. "Those children sure are happy" thought Whiskers. They wanted to pick up the chickens so badly, but they would always run away. And they were so much faster than the children were. When the mother called them in for breakfast, they turned and ran to the house. Leaving the gate open! All three chickens stood as still as they could. Knowing they might realize their mistake and come back to close the pen. But they didn't come back. Whiskers, Little Red, and Buffy looked at each other then made the escape! Out the gate and towards the field. Running as fast as they could, wings flapping all the way. They covered a lot of ground that day, resting and snacking as they went along. Day turned to night. Then the rain started coming down. They found themselves in a wooded area, so that's where they took refuge. Huddling together as they always did, trying to stay warm and dry. But they spent the night being cold and wet.

It was a miserable journey the next morning. They were all wet and had caught a chill. But they kept walking.

Chapter 13

Rocky

After the rainy night, Rocky, Buttons and Dottie emerged from their coop. The three were preening, as they did every morning. They knew Sandy would be out soon with treats. It sure was great being home again. They had settled back into their old routine and weren't as nervous as they were a few days ago. Suddenly Rocky turned his head. "What was that? What did I just hear?" Rocky was standing straight and tall, listening for the sound to repeat itself. That's when Sandy came out with treats in her hand.

THERE IT IS AGAIN!! I know that sound!! Rocky was starting to run back and forth in the pen. Sandy came closer, Rocky was in a panic, Sandy opened the gate and Rocky darted out in a full run. "Rocky! No!! Bad chicken.

You get back here." But Rocky was gone. Running wildly towards the woods. "Oh nooooo" Sandy said. "What on earth has gotten into that rooster?" She laid down the treats and went back inside to get Bill. Maybe between the two of them they could catch him.

Rocky knew that voice, or rather, clucking. It was the love of his life. It was Whiskers! He just knew it. Halfway in the woods, Rocky stopped to listen. Then with all his might, he let out the biggest, longest crow he could do. He waited, but it was just silence. He drew in another breath and let out another loud crow. This time he heard cackling. Loud, fast cackling. Once again, another loud crow and the cackling was returned. Rocky took off running towards the sound. His little heart racing. As he came out the other side of the woods, there she was. His beautiful Whiskers, and Buffy and Little Red. They all ran to each other. Whiskers couldn't believe her eyes. Seeing Rocky was the best thing ever. Rocky did his little dance around the hens then turned and started back, with the girls right behind him. Whiskers was so tired and so wet, she couldn't keep up with the others. Rocky noticed her lagging behind, and he went back to her. Little Red and Buffy were running full out. They knew home was just through those woods.

Chapter 14

The reunion

Bill came out with Sandy to look for Rocky. Buttons and Dottie were still in the pen, but Rocky, for reasons unknow, was gone. Sandy was so furious with herself for letting Rocky get out. She had been though so much the last few weeks. Losing her beloved chickens, finding some of them, wondering where the other three were, and now Rocky getting out. "Hush!" Bill said, holding up his hand. "Did you hear that?" "What?" said Sandy. "Chickens cackling" She held real still, waiting to hear what Bill had heard. That's when Buffy and Little Red came busting out of the woods, running full tilt towards Sandy and Bill. "MY CHICKENS! MY CHICKENS! Bill, look! They've come back!" The two little hens ran right up to Sandy, flapping their wings the whole way. She swooped them up in her arms and started kissing them on their little heads. Then she pulled her head back, looked at them and said, "You're wet!" Bill kept looking towards the woods. "This doesn't make sense. Rocky leaves, and these two come back. So, where's Rocky?" For a moment they both stood looking towards the woods, holding wet chickens, when a big grin started going across Bill's face. Emerging from between the trees were Rocky and Whiskers. Bill pointed at them and said, "Look Sandy! Here comes Whiskers"